Danny to the Rescue

The box is now a transformer. Danny wants to help other people. Read about how he comes to the rescue.

box

Then

jumped

was

Please

people

rescue

late

for

her

don't

stuck

Soon

out

too

it

to

Grandad

will

superhero

them

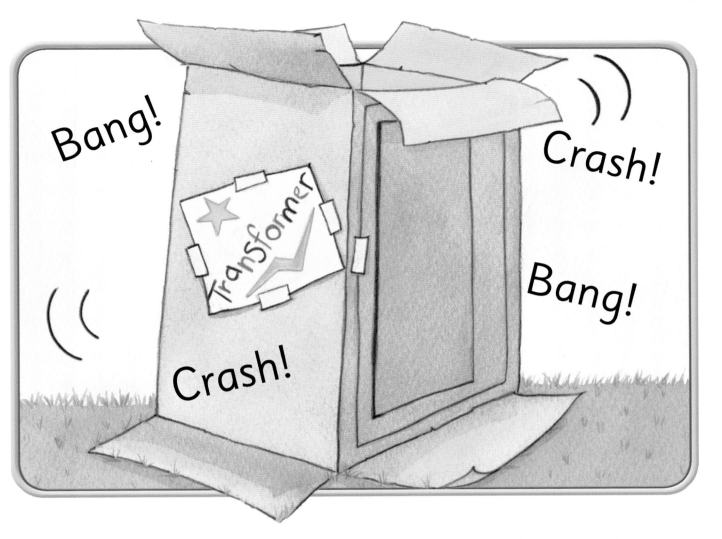

The box went up and down and round
and round!
Then ...

... Danny jumped out.
'I am a superhero,' he said.
'I can help people.'

'Danny to the rescue,' he said,
and off he went.
He looked for people to help.

Soon Danny saw Mum.
'Mum needs help,' said Danny.
'Danny to the rescue,' he said, and off
he went to help her.

'Hello Mum,' said Danny. 'I am a superhero.
I help people and I can help you.'
'Oh no, Danny, no!' said Mum. 'I don't
need help!'
'Please, Danny, don't help,' said Mum ...

... but it was too late!

Soon Danny saw Grandad.
'Grandad needs help,' said Danny.
'Danny to the rescue,' he said, and
off he went to help him.

'Hello Grandad,' said Danny. 'I am
a superhero.
I help people and I can help you.'
'Oh no, Danny, no!' said Grandad.
'I don't need help!'
'Please, Danny, don't help,' said Grandad …

... but it was too late!

Soon Danny saw Zeb.

'Zeb is stuck,' said Danny. 'He needs help and I can help him.'

'Danny to the rescue,' he said, and off he went to help.

Soon Grandad saw Danny and Zeb.
'They need help,' said Grandad. 'I will
help them.'

The box went up and down and round
and round!
Then ...

... Grandad jumped out.
'Grandad to the rescue!' he said, and off
he went to help ...

... but it was too late!

A Snowy Idea

The children are having fun playing in the snow.
Danny has a good idea, but Zeb is not happy,
not happy at all. Read all about Danny's snowy idea.

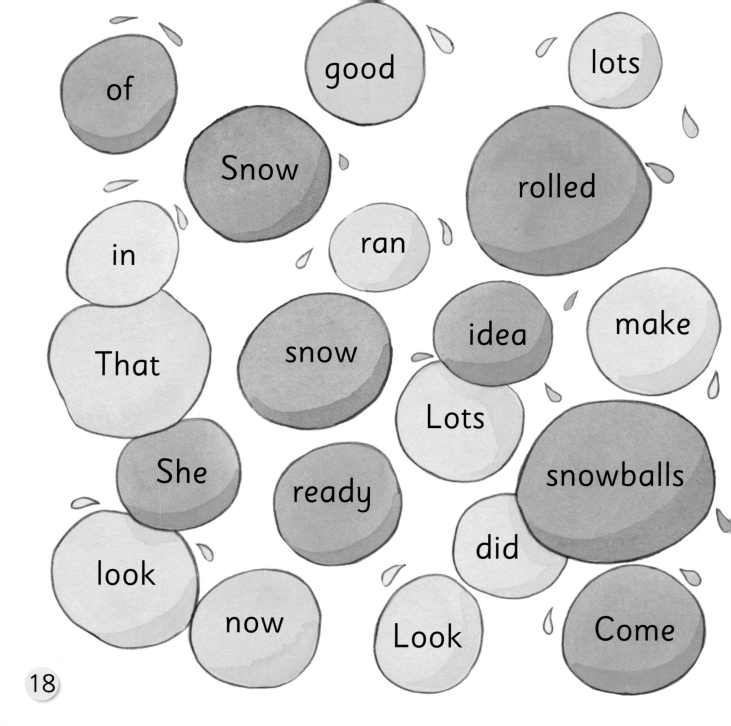

of

good

lots

Snow

rolled

in

ran

That

snow

idea

make

Lots

She

ready

snowballs

look

did

now

Look

Come

18

'Snow!' said Josh.
'Snow!' said Emma. 'Lots and lots of snow!'
'Wow!' said Danny.

Emma and Josh and Danny ran out.
They jumped up and down.
They ran round and round.
They rolled in the snow.
'Snow, snow, lots of snow,' they said.

'I have a good idea,' said Danny.
'We can make snow people,' he said.
'Snow people!' said Emma. 'That is a good idea.'
'Snow people!' said Josh. 'That is a very good idea!'

Danny and Josh and Emma rolled the snow.
They rolled big snowballs.
They rolled lots of them.

They ran in and out.
They ran out and in.
Mum looked at them. She was dizzy.

'I am ready,' said Emma.
'I am ready too,' said Josh.
'Mum, Mum,' said Danny, 'we are
ready. Come out and look at the
snow people.'

'Wow!' said Mum. 'Snow people!
A snow Emma, a snow Josh, and a
snow Danny.'
'That was a very good idea,' she said.

Then Mum looked at Zeb.
'Hello Zeb,' she said. 'Come out and
look at the snow people.'

Zeb looked but he did not look at the snow people.
He looked at a cloud.
He looked at a bird.
He did not look at the snow Emma and the snow Josh.
He did not look at the snow Danny.

'Poor Zeb,' said Danny. 'He is not happy.'
'He is not happy now,' said Mum, 'but
we can make him happy!'
'I have a good idea,' she said.

Mum and Danny and Josh and Emma
rolled the snow.
They rolled big snowballs.
They rolled lots of them.

They ran in and out.
They ran out and in.
Zeb looked at them. He was dizzy.

'We are ready,' they said.
'Look, Zeb, look,' said Danny.
'We have …

... a snow Zeb for you!'